Pieces of Life Between Latitudes

Pieces of Life Between Latitudes

poems by John T. Hitchner

Encircle Publications, LLC
Farmington, Maine USA

Pieces of Life Between Latitudes Copyright ©2015 John T. Hitchner
ISBN 10: 1-893035-25-5
ISBN 13: 978-1-893035-25-6

All rights reserved. No part of this book may be reproduced in any form by any mechanical or electronic means including storage and retrieval systems without express written permission in writing from the publisher. Brief passages may be quoted in review.

Editors: Cynthia Brackett-Vincent and Devin McGuire

Book design: Cynthia Brackett-Vincent
Cover design: Devin McGuire/ENC Graphics Services

Cover photos: Shutterstock.com
Author photo: John R. Hitchner
Printing: Walch Publishing, Portland, Maine

Online Orders:
http://www.encirclepub.com/store/product/pieces-of-life-between-latitudes

Mail Orders, Author Inquiries:
Encircle Publications, LLC
PO Box 187
Farmington, ME USA 04938

Bookstores:
207-778-0467

Acknowledgements

The author wishes to thank the editors of the following journals for publishing the poems listed below, some in slightly different form:

Anthology of New England Writers: "After the Firefight."

The Aurorean: "Driving in November," "Harmony," "Sunrise," "Winter Shadows."

Avocet: "An Epiphany of Stones," "In Prelude," "In the Calm."

The Weekly Avocet: "At Winter Thaw."

Clark Street Review: "In an Airport Waiting Room."

Homestead Review: "Hard Love."

Ink in my Blood: "Sunday Rituals."

Long Story Short: "Bowling Lessons," "Easter Morning."

Slant: "Tending."

* * *

"After the Firefight" received 'Editor's Choice' recognition in the 2004 *Anthology of New England Writers*.

Contents

I. Son and Father
Bowling Lessons 1
Tending 3
Sunday Rituals 4
An Epiphany of Stones 6

II. Brook and Field
Sunrise 11
Harmony 12
In the Fall of the Year 13
In the Calm 14
Do you watch seasons change? 15
In Prelude 16
Winter Shadows 17
A Morning Wonder 18

III. ...and Beyond
Pieces of Life Between Latitudes 23
Boys in Baseball Caps 25
In an Airport Waiting Room 26
Driving in November 27
At Winter Thaw 28
Easter Morning 29
Hard Love 31
After the Firefight 32
In the Winter Shade of Lower Manhattan 33
For You in Our Autumn 34
After the Reception: Things in Their Place 36
Rain 37

About the Author 39

To my grandchildren:

Isabel Grace, Jacob Addis, Kira Danielle, Nora Christine, and Claire Noel

Author Thanks

My sincere thanks to many people for their close reading of my poetry and for their support and friendship. If I have omitted anyone from this list, I sincerely apologize.

First and always, thank you to my wife Pat, my son John, and my step-daughters Kerri Immergut, Kristi Doman, and Amy Janvier for your love and patience. Thank you also to David Aiken, Dawn Andonellis, Cynthia Brackett-Vincent, Jim Bulteel, Randy Burns, David Chase, the late Minette Chatfield, Jack Coey, Bill Derry, Ellen Estabrook, Ray Foreman, Jeff Friedman, Ernest Hebert, Jerry Kaufman, Norman Klein, Jennifer Lagier, Devin McGuire, Sean McElhiney, Kathy Medvidofsky, Ted Miller, Tim Napier, Cara Nichol, Cathy Porter, Charles Portolano, Jay Punt, Charlene Reinbold, Ken Schalhoub, and Jerry Whelan—kind and generous readers all.

I. Son and Father

Bowling Lessons

Again I open a door
and see my father fling his bowling ball—
table lamp smashed to shards,
living room wall a gouged gaping mouth—
late night revenge after strings of splits.

The first time my father and I bowled together
he pressed his fingers
on the tips of my rented shoes
to see if I had enough room—
his touch reassurance.

He stressed alley courtesy,
waiting my turn,
letting the person
in the lane beside me
go first.

His short stature no matter—
arm and leg tendons intense
as smash and tumble of pins,
his follow-through graceful ballet.
Trophies and team pictures upon shelves
brothers and sisters I never had.

Flashes of temper passed with age.
He repaired the wall,
his eyes and fingers precise
as numbers on a score sheet.

Monday night poker replaced
Thursday night bowling—
nickels and dimes in the kitty
small change after singles and fivers on the bar.

In late years
grandchildren held his hands.
My 300 games! he bragged.

Our last game together,
my last roll a split,
his a strike:
his raised fist trophy enough.

Tending

In October
I pull plants from my garden,
pale from first frost.
Lying upon cold soil,
leaves and stalks rest, sleep.
Perhaps they dream
of another season.
I do.

In a season past
I see my grandfather
among inert wooden stakes,
soil from his own garden
slivered beneath his fingernails,
wire stems of his glasses silver
as tufts of hair
at his temples.

I do not ask him
why he always called me
by my nickname,
never my birth name.
I do not ask why he flailed a razor strop
upon my father's childhood legs,
or why he walked footsteps ahead
of my grandmother
to and from church.
It is not my place
to ask such questions now.

My grandfather works content in his garden
of evenly spaced rows,
where poles, stakes, and string
guide life he nourished by hands and water:
a man at peace
with what he can tend.

Sunday Rituals

My father inspects me.
Stand up straight,
You have to look nice for church.
I stiffen, dare not slouch.
He tugs the shoulders, yanks the hem
of my gabardine suit jacket.
Pull your pants higher. Make the creases sharp.
I smell his Old Spice after-shave.
see black whisker specks,
cautious eyebrows.

There, he says, and appraises me:
I guess you look all right.
Behave yourself in church.

I sit beside my mother
in the middle pew.
We watch my father march with the choir,
his hymnal held like an offering.
His throat tightens,
strains for high notes of God's glory.

During prayers I bow my head,
touch the sharp creases of my pants.
No blood shed.
My mother hands me an open prayer book.
I silently read words odd pieces of a puzzle
I've solved every Sunday:
If you say the right words,
God will be happy with you.

What if I ripped and scattered pages
from the prayer book?
Would anyone pick them up,
put them back together?

Stained glass saints and martyrs
stare above my head.
What if I stoned their faces?

Can God see me?
Can He read my mind?
Would He cast me out
or invoke, *Sit up straight! Behave yourself.*

Above us, our minister makes the sign of the Cross:
May the blessing of God the Father, the Son,
and the Holy Spirit be amongst you
and remain with you, always.

My mother bows her head,
folds her hands.
My father cradles his hymnal.
My hands skim creases of my pants,
like fingers testing blades of knives.

An Epiphany of Stones

It came to me
to feel the stones once more
beneath my feet,
smooth my fingers
across their cognizant runes.
Long ago the stones surrendered
beneath a father's footsteps.
Long ago the stones yielded
to a child's shy curiosity,
allowed the child to hold, smell,
taste cold surfaces wrought
by eons of wind and rain.
Beyond childhood curiosity now
a man sees the stones have not truly aged,
but still carry scents of garage grease and oil,
elements handed down in lessons
of how things work and knowing a child's place.

And it came to me
to consider the tools
fast upon brackets and shelves:
drivers, pliers, hammers, wrenches—
utensils, like children, in proper places then,
relics under invisible glass now;
possessions without soul then,
providers of the shape of life now.

For what is a revisit of stones,
metal, and wood
but new perspective?
We focus into clarity
scents of cigars and flannel,
grease and oil,
and the presence of an ignored
but curious child.

What is it but ourselves
we believe we know,
only to learn surface and scent
is not all we see?
It is not everything.

II. Brook and Field

Sunrise

Sunrise crests East Hill
and wakes the city.
Stones at brook bottom
shimmer secrets.

Not far from here long ago,
bear and deer roamed through
birch, poplar, and hemlock.
Grouse thrummed wings upon paths
in pride of territory.

This morning, all are gone;
hunting trails now paths to fenced yards,
birches, poplar, hemlock chain-sawed out.
Young trees stand wary of disease.

Still, the brook's stones know
the beaver's paths and dens,
and watch a gray heron's cautious steps.
And still on warm spring evenings
we see first star and crescent moon
above East Hill:
promises of sunrise.

Harmony

A sun-clouded morning
of another autumn;
time out of balance
between harvest home
and giving thanks.
Sky and absent snow
memories of old storms
and hope for a new year.

Here, though, along the brook
stays the natural harmony of white birches—
old friends who ask for nothing,
want for nothing,
only the hope, perhaps,
they feel the first snowfall
settle on their arms.

In the Fall of the Year

In the fall of the year
high wind and rain
whirled in clouds across the field.
Under sun the next morning
we walked the field,
grass stubble underfoot
stern preparation for snow.
White birches bent before white hemlock
in casual dare for sun.
We paid homage to a burning bush,
flameless, voiceless, and alone
at a stone wall as if cast out—
By force of nature?
Divine intervention?
And we marveled at the fortitude
of the stones,
those that wall in secrets,
and those that endure what felled trees
honored what came before.

In the Calm

In the month before Christmas,
holly berries seem scarlet rubies
along this woodland path above the brook,
and yellow maple leaves
curl like cold hands
upon cold ground.

Perhaps it is the sun's lowering eye,
more likely my own body's aging clock,
but I've never felt more close,
yet more distant from the world.

Newspapers spill another suicide attack
in an unwinnable war.
Talking heads hawk political slander
even Lyndon Johnson would demand,
Where is Reason?
Where is Calm?

Time lies brittle as buried bones.
In late autumn,
no fires burn,
no blood spills.
Here in this calm
our arms must learn to love again

Do you watch seasons change?

Why that song?
Why your voice?
I do not hear the words,
only the melody's long-ago past.

How did we transgress?

Beyond an old New England house
one season ends,
another begins.
Radios carol another Christmas,
jingles jangle presents to buy.

Do you watch seasons change?

I watch brook water shine in sunlight.
I wait earth to soften,
track storms,
watch trees sway.

Do you see the same sky,
hear the same song?
Do you, like me, wait for seasons
to change?

In Prelude

In prelude to a season of goodwill,
brook water shines upon stones.
The current folds upon itself,
a lover enacting a ritual
rain and snow will nourish,
and only ice will hide
until melting season releases passion again.
The pull of the moon,
the run of the earth
will grant eternal blessing.

Winter Shadows

Raw December:
Snow bursts speckle meadow grass,
and sprinkle tiny beads
upon the brook current
that swirls them away,
the bottom in sunlight
a cold shimmer of pebbles and sand.

As I walk the brook path,
I watch my shadow
upon the water,
a dark silhouette that passes,
unlike as in life,
smoothly over stones.

A Morning Wonder

On a mild winter morning
trees and roofs weep snowmelt.
What will become of those drops
after they fall to old snow?
Will earth accept them
at spring equinox?
Will they nourish perennials?
Or, will wind and rain
wash them to streams and seas,
then carry them high to clouds
so that some mild day we,
like the children our hearts sing for,
will feel them, cradle them in our hands,
and marvel at their coming again?

III. …and Beyond

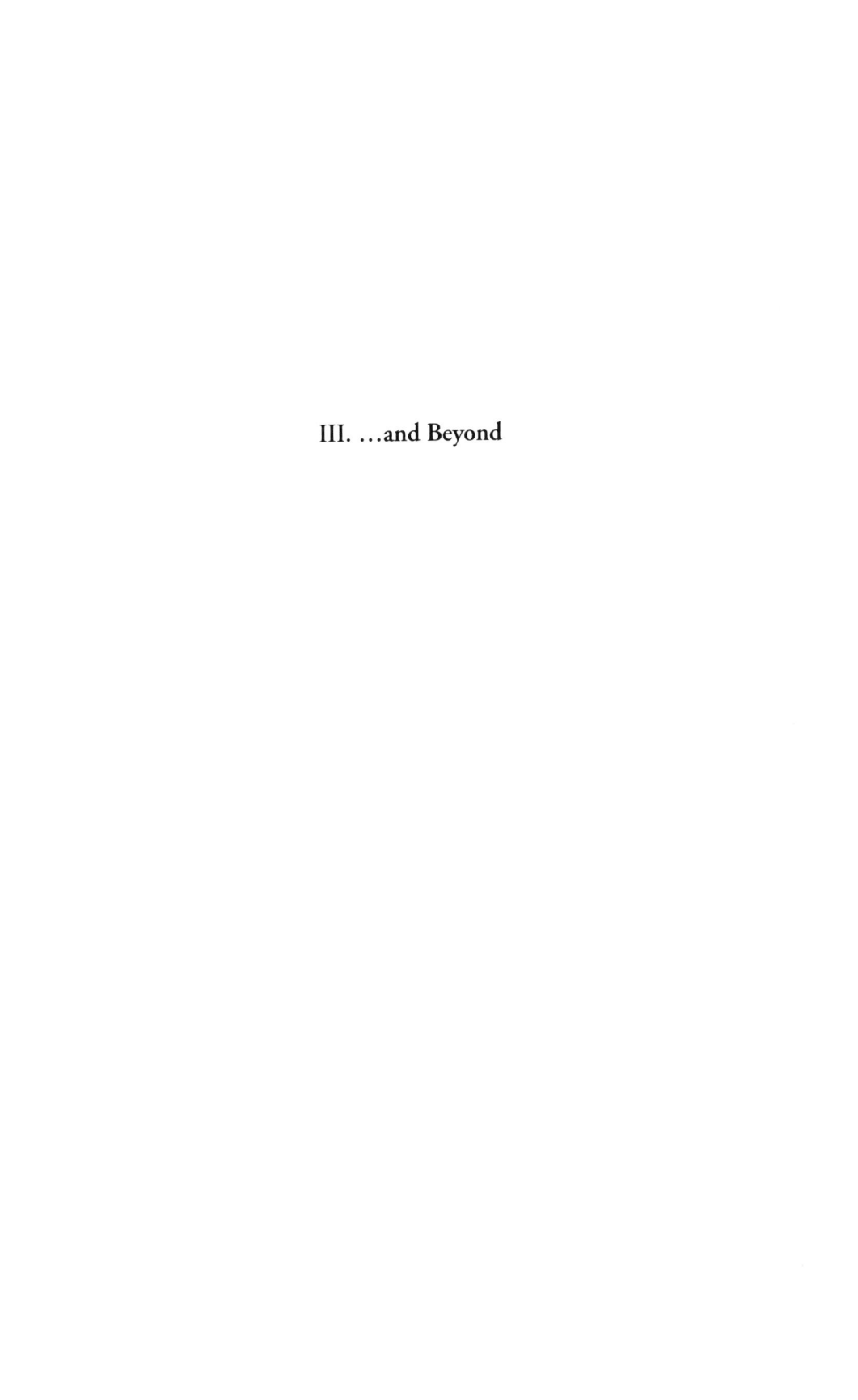

Pieces of Life Between Latitudes

1.

I live between middle and northern latitudes:
seven pills at breakfast,
five at lunch,
one before bed.
Fitness experts never seem to age,
do they.

2.

Each day I listen to show tunes.
I live love found and lost,
trespasses unforgiven,
reconciliation without grace.
Rain upon the roof never enough
to drown consequences.

3.

Plaque strangled my father's brain.
He did not, could not, read.
He turned pages as if looking
for some thing, some one,
to tell him my name.

4.

Lover, who's that on the phone?
Why do you turn away and lower your voice?
Are *Yes* and *No* code?
Our forsythia and lilac branches crisscross
like friends who search for sun.
Not finding it,
they turn upon themselves.

5.

Even as clouds reveal and hide the sun,
trees—ancestors who remember the Past—
shadow the ground and foretell the future.

Boys in Baseball Caps

Boys in baseball caps
cast down stones upon rocks
at the edge of the bay.
Their father watches,
a casual form against the horizon.
Flung stones spike
from rocks to water,
each rock a face bruised,
an eye blinded,
a bone broken.
Yet, the attack propels
ceaseless, hopeless, reasonless,
for hope is not the solution,
reason not the motive,
only the innate decision to hurl a weapon,
raise a fist in pride of attack
while a father stands by,
watches,
and does not speak.

In an Airport Waiting Room

I stand at a window
and watch planes arrive and depart,
fuselages sleek,
dark windows blind to earth and sky.

That 747 lifting off now—
its wings sway, test resistance,
cut current hawks and eagles glide within.
A higher altitude gained by us,
another machined wind beaten down upon them.

What do we seek
above canyons and mountains,
rivers and oceans?
A space closer to God?
Someplace other than home?
No promise fulfilled,
except arrive somewhere soon as possible,
or compare spreadsheet numbers,
or possess more of what controls us.
One could do more than be
a passenger on a plane.

Driving in November

October's colors drift in wind
like broken promises,
hillside trees unclothed,
scarred and slashed by storms.
I drive tonight in November.

I've traveled this road before
into April's false spring,
June's melancholy solstice,
and September's early autumn.
This November night
I drive between seasons—
harvest home,
gifts forgotten,
prayers unspoken.
Hillside houselights few,
long spaces between
like empty inches on a map,
where only words unforgiven live.

At Winter Thaw

On a day of winter thaw
I open doors and windows
and welcome new air and morning light.
Rooms where we live
taste sudden cool air.
Our children and grandchildren
in picture frames
hold wedding day and grade school smiles.
Even you and I above the fireplace mantle
show youth and hope in newfound love.

Beyond the west windows,
the oak tree's low limbs
clutch caramel-brown leaves,
unwilling to yield to the natural course
of birth, growth, disintegration.
Unlike other trees,
perhaps this old rebel lives by its own rules:
unfold, withhold, stay.
Or perhaps it mocks us—
we who follow the path others have lived:
trial and error, gains and losses.

Now a northwest wind
only tremors the oak's leaves
and foretells greater cold.
Tracks of squirrels and birds
will freeze in place
until smothered by new powder.

I close the doors, shut windows,
and stoke the fire,
ordinary tasks that comfort the heart
and postpone the inevitable.

Easter Morning

My son calls home
from two thousand miles east
of Old Jerusalem and the Place of Skulls.
He does not speak of scripture
or denials or revelations,
nor does he agonize
over IEDs, RPGs, or bomb-belted avengers.

He reassures me that where he is
the food is good,
security tight,
care packages and well wishes
arrived appreciated and intact.
He allows that he and friends
gathered hours ago for sunrise service
within the zone, behind the wire.

As we talk, even laugh,
I watch a cloud of memories,
precise as driven nails,
pass across the sun.
I see him cradled in my arms,
hear the swish of a basketball net
after *nothin' but net!*
I feel the taut wait for his car
in the driveway after a concert in the city,
I smell oily exhaust
from the bus that carried him
and fellow recruits to Boot Camp.

Before the conversation deadline,
I ask, *Are you all right?*
Is there anything you need?

Easter sunlight shades window curtains.
I am thankful for such cool light,
and thankful even more for my son's voice
thousands of miles away from my own,
a distance, yes,
but one not as great and lasting
as blood and sorrows other crusades
have wrought upon the world.

Hard Love

Where are words of natural affection?
In tremble of windows?
In tumble of flesh and bone
across wood and stone?
Where?

On paper
words offer cold comfort,
thin as smoke,
empty as a lover's hand drawn away.
The heart demands comfort hard,
truth hard as fist upon face,
as bruise upon heart.
The heart demands your palms open
to hold my face,
your hand never break my heart again.
These are my words.
Are they enough?

After the Firefight

It was a wail in the wind.

It was a room
without lamps and pictures,
without tables and chairs.
It was a bed without frame,
music without melody,
a clock without hands.
It was a prayer without words,
a chalice without wine,
a body without blood.

It was the lion in the car.
The car in flames,
and bodies on the bridge.
It was the knife at the throat,
the sword at the neck,
the bayonet at the heart,
the hands in the street,
and it was the helmet upon the rifle.

It was the coffin.
It was the flag upon the coffin,
and the rose upon the coffin,
and the hand upon the coffin,
and the kiss upon the coffin,
and questions in the air above the coffin.

It was, it was,
and it is.

In the Winter Shade of Lower Manhattan

I climb stairs to sidewalks
where dust and ash
no longer fester in metal grates,
where fences no longer rim the pit,
and where notes, phone numbers and photographs
no longer beg answers.
Vendors hawk cones of flowers,
and the banner at St. Paul's Chapel proclaims
Peace Is Our Mission.

In the streets
a soundtrack of ordinary noise plays again.
Taxis complain,
trucks maneuver deliveries,
people text and confirm appointments.

I see no children.
Where are the children?

They do not read plaques
that honor fallen firefighters and police.
They do not read names on metal plates
above the Memorial Garden pools.
Perhaps we survivors do not bring children
to the place once of rubble, cries, and loss,
now of stone, steel, and glass.
Perhaps the children pursue enemies
and broker peace at home.

Are plaques and names enough?
Will the towers be high enough?

What will voices of those we lost
tell us when, somehow, somewhere,
they see our tributes?
We must decide
before we build another monument.

We must decide for the children.

For You in Our Autumn

I smooth my fingers across a fallen maple leaf,
one of a montage of leaves—
orange, red, yellow, and umber
upon our frost-tipped lawn.

Remember how we kicked through leaves
on our walks home with the kids?

I sweep pine needles from the deck.
Remembering those first snows of our cabined years,
I carry two Adirondack chairs inside, where,
together, we will sip warm tea
within our room of books and your paintings
of spring and summer landscapes.

Remember how we read Marlowe and Dickinson
to each other,
I your passionate shepherd,
you my lover rowing in Eden.

But I cannot ask you anymore
To whisper my name
Or to swim those waters.

And so I give you prescribed daily dosage,
but those pills won't dissolve
the snakes of plaque strangling your memory.

I watch you stare at the television screen.
You don't smile anymore,
you don't laugh anymore
at the chummy neighbors and bumbling policemen.

Your mouth struggles for words ordinary
as a child's questions,
and your eyes wonder like a wordless infant
trying to understand faces above a crib.

And so I roam room to room,
smooth curtains, talk to photographs
of you and me and our children.
Then, together again, we watch the sunset
lose color and light beyond West Hill.
Our hill, our paths.
Remember?

After the Reception: Things in Their Place

The porch without chairs,
a house of empty chairs with empty arms.

A house with walls,
empty walls of frameless rectangles and squares,
where light once captured us,
our children,
and your watercolors—
lilies asleep on a pond,
morning glories enfolded upon a trellis.

A house of stairs without footsteps,
without the shadow of light from our bedroom,
the bed without you, your arm a crescent across the pillow.

Our bedroom without laughter,
without sighs,
without breath.
After breath, silence,
and after silence, the search for words.

Rain

Rain: fall upon us,
cleanse ponds and brooks,
streets and sidewalks,
and houses of brick, stone, and wood.

Fall upon the house
where we made tents of blankets,
raised our children,
and laid fires.

Fall upon the house
where I played games,
read books, came of age,
and lived lives of love and war.

Rain: fall upon us,
nourish our hearts,
grace our souls,
and make us clean for all our tomorrows.

About the Author

John T. "Jack" Hitchner grew up in Pitman, New Jersey, and graduated from Glassboro State College (now Rowan University) and Dartmouth College. He also studied at the University of Bath in the United Kingdom. For over thirty years he taught English in public schools in New Jersey and New Hampshire. He lives with his wife Pat in Keene, New Hampshire, where he is adjunct professor of Coming of Age in War and Peace and Creative Writing at Keene State College.

He is the author of the poetry chapbooks *Not Far From Here*, and *Seasons and Shadows*, the short story collection *How Far Away, How Near*, and the novel *The Acolyte*.